Title - Earth, Wind, Water, & Fire
ISBN 13 - 978-1-955144-06-3
Composer - Andrew T Hanna
Graphic Design, Layout, & Artwork - Andrew T Hanna
Copyright - 2022
Genre - Jazz/Bebop/Post-Bop

Earth, Wind, Water, and Fire was composed during my sophomore year at The University of the Arts some time in 1999. When my sophomore year arrived, the limitations of jazz became apparent. Some of which was the lack of different forms, meters, harmonies, rhythms, melodic structure, and the use of counter melodies. Realizing these limitations, whether by synergy or dumb luck, sometime that year, a class assignment was given to make an original arrangement of a jazz standard. On Green Dolphin Street was chosen and arranged for 4 horns - alto, tenor, and baritone saxophone and trumpet. It is uncertain if that arrangement still exists, but that arrangement served as one of two inspirational sources for Earth, Wind, Water, and Fire. The second inspirational source for this song was John Coltrane's interpretation of Mongo Santamara's Afro Blue.

Knowing the inspiration for Earth, Wind, Water, and Fire, the musical elements of this song comprises of 4 repeating counter melodies with the 5th melody performed over top. Rhythmically, the piano and bass outline the 3/8 meter, while the tenor saxophone has a repeating 5 bar melody, and the soprano saxophone has a melody that lasts 5 beats. Harmonically, it is based on a repeating Db Lydian cadence.

In the end, I hope you enjoy performing this as much as the musicians who performed it.

Until next time.

Andrew Hanna

Earth, Wind, Water, & Fire

Andrew Hanna

10
Sop. Sax.
Ten. Sax.
Al. Sax
Pno.
Bass
Dr.
3
15
Sop. Sax.
Ten. Sax.
Al. Sax
Pno.
Bass
Dr.
3

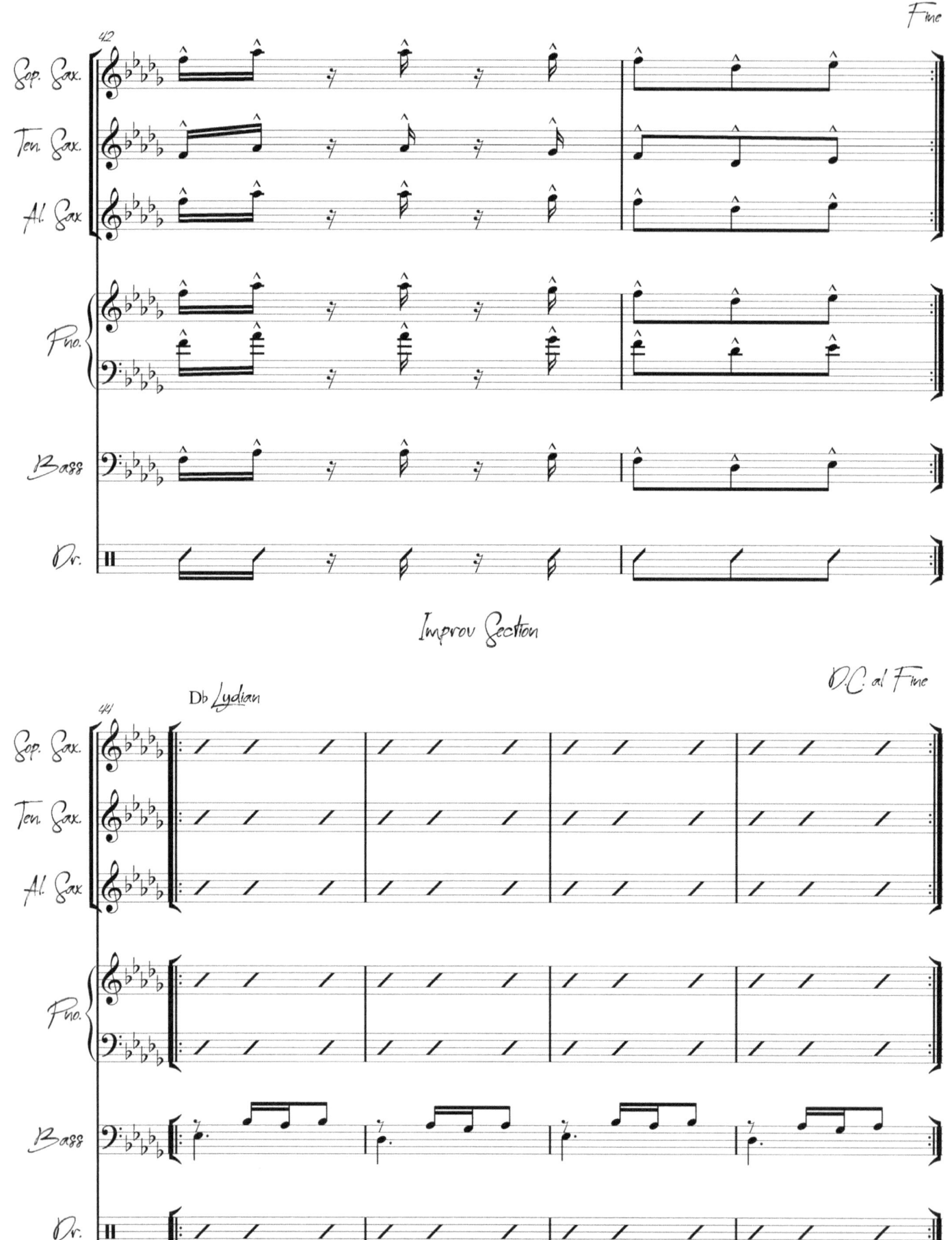

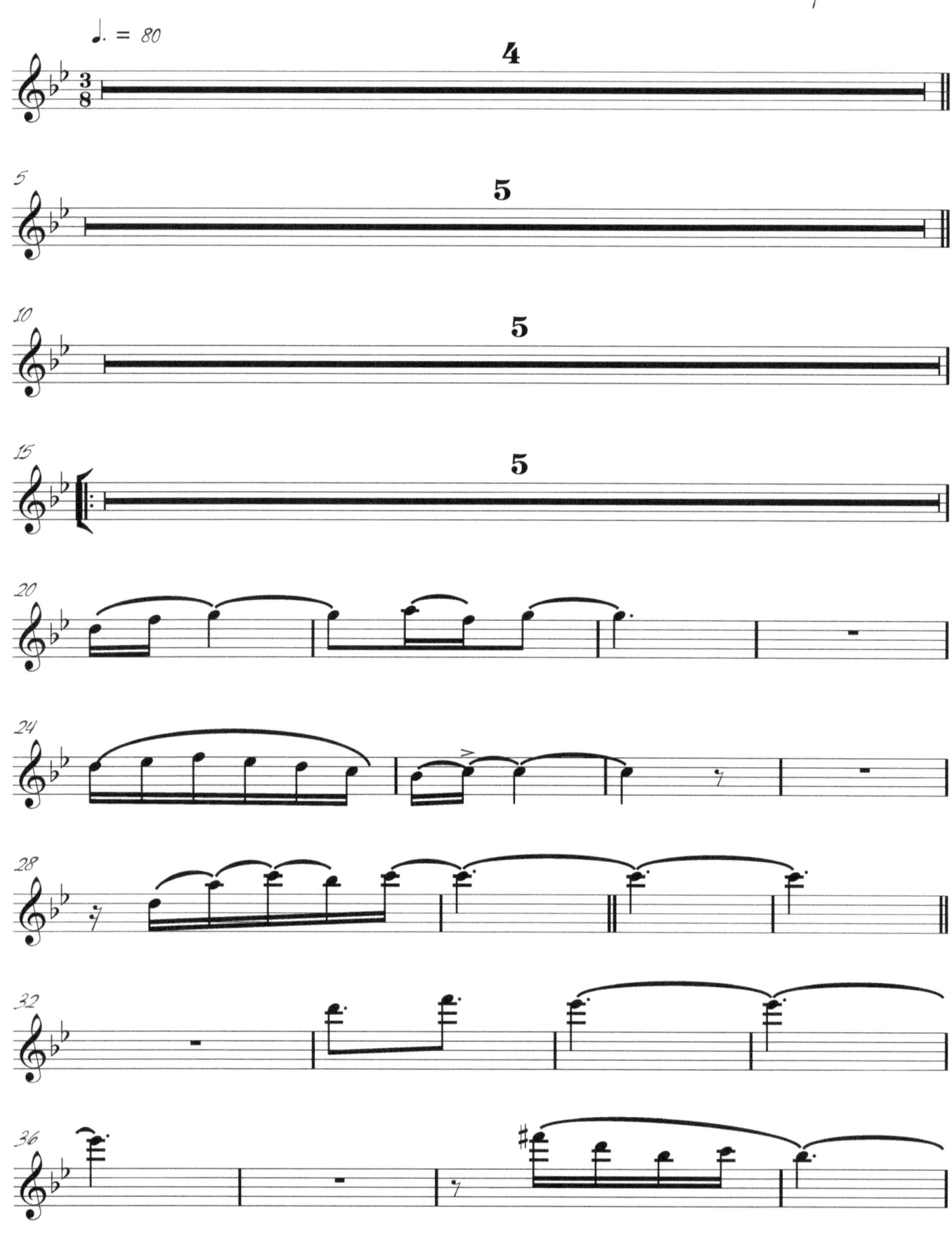

Earth, Wind, Water, & Fire

Tenor Saxophone

Andrew Hanna

Earth, Wind, Water, & Fire

Electric Bass

Andrew Hanna

Earth, Wind, Water, & Fire

Drum Set

Andrew Hanna

♩. = 80

www.ingramcontent.com/pod-product-compliance
Lightning Source LLC
Chambersburg PA
CBHW082041080526
44578CB00009B/799